McFarlin Library
WITHDRAWN

27: Latin America in the World System: The Limits of Internationalism

THE WASHINGTON PAPERS
Volume III

27: Latin America in the World System: The Limits of Internationalism

James D. Theberge

THE CENTER FOR STRATEGIC AND INTERNATIONAL STUDIES
Georgetown University, Washington, D.C.

SAGE PUBLICATIONS
Beverly Hills / London

University of Tulsa
McFarlin Library
Tulsa, Okla.

Copyright © 1975 by
The Center for Strategic and International Studies
Georgetown University

Printed in the United States of America

All rights reserved. No part of this book may be reproduced
or utilized in any form or by any means, electronic or mechanical,
including photocopying, recording, or by any
information storage and retrieval system, without permission in writing
from the publisher.

For information address:

SAGE PUBLICATIONS, INC.
275 South Beverly Drive
Beverly Hills, California 90212

SAGE PUBLICATIONS LTD
St George's House / 44 Hatton Garden
London EC1N 8ER

International Standard Book Number 0-8039-0571-8

Library of Congress Catalog Card No. 75-22729

FIRST PRINTING

When citing a Washington Paper, please use the proper form. Remember to cite the series title and include the paper number. One of the two following formats can be adapted (depending on the style manual used):

(1) HASSNER, P. (1973) "Europe in the Age of Negotiation." The Washington Papers, I, 8. Beverly Hills and London: Sage Pubns.

OR

(2) Hassner, Pierre. 1973. *Europe in the Age of Negotiation.* The Washington Papers, vol. 1, no. 8. Beverly Hills and London: Sage Publications.

CONTENTS

	Foreward	
I.	Latin American Integration and Cooperation	3
II.	Relations with the Pacific Region	9
III.	Relations with Japan	13
IV.	Relations with Canada	17
V.	Relations with Western Europe	21
	Map	26
VI.	Relations with the Soviet Union, Eastern Europe, and China	27
VII.	Relations with the Third World	33
VIII.	Food Production	37
IX.	Mineral Raw Materials Production	41
X.	Latin America as World Oil Supplier	45
XI.	Conventional Arms Transfer	49
XII.	Nuclear Technology Transfer	53
XIII.	The Limits of Internationalism	59
	Notes	63
	References	65

FOREWORD

Latin America's integration into the world political and economic system, a process that began five centuries ago with the European discovery and conquest of the New World, has intensified and assumed new forms since the end of World War II. The vigorous striving for national economic development, the upsurge of economic nationalism, and the decline in East-West tensions in the sixties and seventies have provided a powerful impetus to the spinning of a complex web of political and economic relationships between the Latin American republics and regions of the world remote from the traditional North Atlantic area. This global readjustment of relations, with closer alignment with other developing countries as a prominent feature, will become a major new focus of Latin American politics during the final quarter of this century.

This essay focuses on some important dimensions of Latin America's new and deepening relationships with areas of the world—Asia, Africa, the Middle East, the Pacific Basin, and the socialist camp—where ties scarcely existed before, and on certain special links between the Latin American region and the world markets for arms, nuclear technology, food, and energy. It examines some of the significant domestic and international factors that have provided the impetus for this diversification and intensification of relations. In the concluding section, some of the causes and limitations of this process of global integration are suggested.

One naturally approaches with some trepidation the task of writing an essay that attempts to portray the increasingly broader, more complex role that Latin America is playing in the world system. As we know, the term "Latin America" masks enormous regional disparities in race, culture, education, population, geography, industrialization, ideology, and power. Anyone who discusses Latin America runs the obvious risk of gross oversimplification and empty generalization.

It is also impossible within this space to give adequate consideration to the many political and economic issues inexorably connected with the process of regional incorporation into the world system. All that one can do is to touch on some of the main issues and identify some of the major forces at work. By definition, an essay is a limited exercise in the interpretation of events and trends, and not everyone can be expected to agree with the conclusions set forth here. In any case, it is my hope that it will stimulate others to add to our knowledge of a topic of increasing importance to the countries of the Western Hemisphere—a topic that has not received the attention that it now clearly merits.

The author wishes to express his indebtedness to those many experts, too numerous to mention, whose works and insights were so helpful in the preparation of this essay. In particular, he would like to mention Miguel Wionczek, Lawrence Krause, John Harbron, John Redick, Joseph Grunwald, William Tyler, Roger Fontaine, and Hiroya Ichikawa. It must be emphasized, however, that the views expressed herein are the sole responsibility of the author.

J.D.T.

I. LATIN AMERICAN ECONOMIC INTEGRATION AND COOPERATION

After World War II, there was an enormous increase of interest in promoting the economic integration of national economies in Western Europe and elsewhere through the abolishment of discrimination among the economic units of different national states.[1] In Western Europe alone, the Benelux customs union, the European Coal and Steel Community, the European Economic Community, and the European Free Trade Area were launched. This interest in economic integration soon spread to Latin America where the Central American Common Market and the Latin American Free Trade Association were created in 1960. Subsequently, sub-regional integration movements led to agreements establishing sub-regional common markets in Central America, the Andean area, and the Caribbean. After nearly two decades of experimentation, however, Latin American efforts to integrate national economies on a region-wide basis have proven to be largely illusory. Moreover, it is not likely that wider Latin American economic integration will be achieved in the foreseeable future, if ever. Vested interests, indifference of the larger regional powers, fears by the smaller countries of reaping unequal benefits, and national rivalries, present formidable obstacles.

Even Latin American economic cooperation has been weak and sporadic. Thus far, despite repeated efforts, it has not been possible to create a viable, Latin American organization capable of regular coordination of a regional position on the major issues of trade, finance, and development. The Special Commission for Latin American Coordination (CECLA), established in May 1969 at the Viña del Mar Conference, was set up to produce a common policy position vis a vis the United States at regular OAS (Organization of American States) meetings. CECLA was not given a permanent organizational structure and met on an ad hoc basis to discuss issues of regional interest. While achieving some common positions—notably in September 1971, when Special Commission members issued a protest against the U.S. 10 percent surcharge on all U.S. imports—CECLA soon fell into neglect and disuse as members found policy coordination difficult and time-consuming.

More recently, Mexico and Venezuela have taken the initiative to create a new regional organization—the Latin American Economic System (SELA)—to provide a forum to discuss common problems and establish common positions vis a vis the industrial countries and the multinational corporations. According to the joint declaration of March 1975, signed by Presidents Luis Echevarria of Mexico and Carlos Andres Perez of Venezuela, SELA aims at the defense of prices and markets for Latin American raw materials and manufactures, the establishment of Latin American multinational companies, and the fostering of regional financial, technical, and scientific cooperation.

But SELA is far from enjoying the backing of all the Latin American countries, some of which believe the Mexico-Venezuelan effort is politically motivated and lacks seriousness of purpose. Others fear that SELA will become a weapon of confrontation with the United States and achieve nothing of substance. Thus, SELA may prove to be only another empty symbolic gesture to heighten Latin American interest in continental unity and integration. In any event, it is doubtful that SELA will be more successful than previous efforts to create a Latin American economic organization of consultation and cooperation, but it is still too early to judge.

Latin American political and economic disunity is not the result of the divisive maneuvers of the multinational companies or "U.S. imperialism", as is sometimes falsely alleged. The lack of unity is partly due to the fact that the region is composed of countries with varying levels of income and development, ruled by rival ideologies with competing rather than complementary economies, and encumbered by an inadequate (but improving) regional transport and communications infrastructure. It is also partly the result of historical rivalries and suspicions as well as real conflicts of political and economic interest that exist among the Latin American countries, which cannot be disguised by repeated protestations of Latin solidarity and unity. Furthermore, personal rivalries and leadership ambitions of certain Latin American heads of states constitute another persistent obstacle to wider regional economic integration and cooperation.

The four major, competitive centers of political influence and economic strength—Argentina, Brazil, Mexico, and Venezuela—pose significant barriers to regional political and economic cohesion. Each major Latin American power believes it is large enough (or rich enough in Venezuela's case) to secure by itself the basis for its own national economic integration and development. Each of these power centers has created, or is creating, its own sphere of influence in adjacent geographic areas.

Argentina has been locked in competition with Brazil for influence in the southern zone *(el cono sur)* of South America since the nineteenth century, although it is only relatively recently that Argentina has come to take Brazil's historical territorial, demographic, and economic expansion seriously. Argentina's chronic political instability, social conflict, and poor economic management has reduced its ability to act decisively in its competition with Brazil in regional and world affairs.

At present, Brazil is the only country in the region with the economic strength, political cohesion, and resource base to conduct a serious, sustained regional and global foreign policy. Brazil is confident of its national identity and destiny, and appears capable of overcoming the oil crisis with its extraordinary recent economic growth performance largely unimpaired. Brazil's $70 billion GNP, 100 million population, and rapid expansion of industry and foreign trade are, however, creating a power imbalance in South America that causes concern in neighboring countries. Over the past decade, heavy investment in major hydro-electric and irrigation projects on the upper Parana River, including joint projects with Paraguay and Uruguay, has created tension and conflict with a less dynamic Argentina. Furthermore, Brazil's economic and demographic penetration of neighboring Argentina and Bolivia has aroused jealousies and fears of Brazilian expansion.

Among the Andean countries, Peru is particularly concerned about Brazil's growing economic power. Peru's anti-capitalist and anti-Western military dictatorship is antagonistic to Brazil's pro-West, anti-communist military government which has made enormous strides in industrialization. In contrast, the radical, anti-capitalist path to development adopted by the Peruvian military has failed to win widespread popular allegiance and shows signs of economic decline with productivity falling as state ownership and control expand. The six-nation Andean community[2] was established at least in part as a defensive economic alliance and Spanish-speaking counterweight to Brazil's rapid economic expansion.

In Mexico, President Echevarria's foreign policy is designed to diversify Mexico's political and economic relations, to reduce economic dependence on the United States, and to convert Mexico into a force in Third World politics. Mexico also has been extending its relations with the countries of the Caribbean basin and Central America. It is precisely this diplomatic activism and the growing Mexican economic presence in the Caribbean-Central American area that provokes suspicion and fear on the part of the smaller, weaker countries within Mexico's sphere of influence. Despite the radical foreign policy postures taken by the government to pacify the Mexican left, there are signs of increasing domestic pressures to reform what local critics call the PRI (Institutional Revolutionary Party) system of interlocking political cliques *(camarillas)* that receive a disproportionate share of the benefits of the Mexican system. The erosion of the PRI's legitimacy, the crisis of the *ejido* system, the rural poverty and widespread unemployment, the demographic explostion and strains on the educational system may well compel the Mexican government to focus more attention on domestic problems during the next Presidential period which begins in 1976.

Venezuela has obviously benefited greatly from its OPEC membership, but at the expense of the net oil-importing countries of Latin America (particularly in Central America and the Caribbean) whose balance of payments have suffered due to the fourfold increase in oil prices in 1972-1974. Criticism by these countries has been blunted by Venezuela's policy of promising help to form other OPEC-type cartels for other mineral and tropical commodity exports and by recycling surplus petro-dollars to the Central American countries, Jamaica, the World Bank, the Inter-American Development Bank (IDB), and the United Nations.

Nevertheless, with the decline in prices for many Latin American mineral and tropical commodity exports since the end of 1974 and the OPEC policy of upward adjustment of oil prices, this latent source of conflict between regional oil-importing and oil-exporting countries (particularly Venezuela and Ecuador) already is beginning to surface. For example, in April 1975, the Colombian government criticized both the oil-exporting and the industrial countries for "victimizing" the states that must import oil and manufactured goods, whose prices have been sharply increased over the past few years. The industrial oil-importing countries are able to compensate for the oil price increase by raising the prices of their manufactured exports, something the less developed oil-importing countries cannot do.

In the mid-1970s, Mexico and Venezuela have begun to pursue parallel foreign policies. Both countries are attempting to create a *New International Economic Order* that would include the indexation of raw material prices, the creation of producer cartels, the recovery of national sovereignty over natural resources, the regulation of multinational companies, and the control of the transfers of technology. The "new order" aims at a massive redistribution of world income from the developed to the less developed countries under the guise of improving the Third World terms of trade.

Many of these foreign policy initiatives are criticized within Latin America as incoherent and contradictory. It is doubtful, for example, whether the ambitious and improvised proposals to cartelize international trade in mineral and tropical commodities will enjoy any significant or lasting success. Venezuela's effort to support a Central American coffee producers cartel has already failed.

Thus, the achievement of regional political or economic cohesion faces immense obstacles. The only exception to this rule involves regional solidarity in a dispute with the United States (such as siding with Panama in the Canal dispute and opposing restrictive commodity and OPEC clauses in the 1974 U.S. Trade Act).

The effective political integration of the Latin American countries is even more difficult to bring about than the marshalling of regional economic cooperation or the establishment of a free trade area or common market. It would require a substantial surrender of sovereignty to a regional supranational organization that is clearly in conflict with the rising tide of Latin American nationalism. Bonds of a common culture, language, and history do not necessarily provide an adequate basis for successful regional economic cooperation and in particular for the more advanced stages of economic and political integration.

More favorable prospects for regional economic cooperation and integration reside in the creation of a series of sub-regional political-economic groups with restricted membership, such as the Andean Community, the Central American Common Market, and the Caribbean Common Market. Policy coordination and economic cooperation is more manageable among smaller groups of nations of similar economic strength that face common domestic and foreign policy problems. But these partial, less ambitious steps towards greater intra-regional integration and cooperation also must overcome serious political and economic conflicts that emerge between member states (such as the hostilities between El Salvador and Honduras in Central America and the dispute over the foreign investment code and industrial sector programming within the Andean Group). The central question for the future is whether even these sub-regional political-economic groups will be able to create sufficient political cohesion and solidarity to overcome the centrifugal nationalisms of their member states.

II. RELATIONS WITH THE PACIFIC REGION

Latin America's trade, investment, and technology links with the Pacific region, which comprises Oceania and all countries bordering the Pacific Ocean in Asia, plus Canada, have been growing steadily over the past decade. Within this regional constellation, three countries—Japan, Canada, and Australia—form the fourth most dynamic subsector of the world economy, after the United States, the European Economic Community, and the European socialist bloc. Japan's GNP alone trails behind only that of the United States and the Soviet Union.

Commercial exchange between these major Pacific trading nations and Latin America is still of marginal importance, although Japan is rapidly emerging as a major new economic partner for some Latin American countries. Trade with the Pacific region amounted to about 10 percent of total Latin American trade in 1970, two-thirds of which was with Japan and just under one-third with Canada. The single most important obstacle to an expansion of Latin America's trans-Pacific trade is the limited and imperfect knowledge in Latin America of the economic, resource, and technological developments taking place in Australia, Canada, Japan, and the lesser Western Pacific countries.

A common denominator among the major Pacific nations and Latin America is the strong upsurge of economic nationalism in recent years that has stimulated a desire to diversify relations and seek new markets in the Pacific region. Canada and Australia, in particular, share the aim of many Latin American countries to strengthen the regulation and control of multinational corporations so as to avoid foreign domination of key sectors of the economy and to insure that they provide needed capital, technology, and management skills on more favorable terms.

Development assistance to Latin America from the Pacific nations is negligible and is unlikely to become more important in the future despite the rapid rise in total official economic aid from Japan, Australia, and Canada since the end of the sixties. Most of Japan's official capital and technical assistance continues to be channeled to its Asian neighbors; Australian aid is almost entirely absorbed in Papua-New Guinea and Southeast Asia; and Canadian aid to the Pacific coast Latin American countries is minor, but rising.

The major obstacles to trans-Pacific trade relations are the dramatic expansion of resource-base industries in the Western Pacific and Canada and the lack of complementarity between Latin America and the remaining parts of the Pacific region. At present, Chilean and Peruvian metals, for example, cannot easily compete in the Japanese market with the more accessible wealth of Australia and adjacent areas. This situation is already beginning to change, however, since Japan is making an intensified effort to diversify and insure the stability of its sources of raw material supply. The inefficiency of highly protected Latin American industries will continue to hinder the export of manufactured goods to other parts of the Pacific region even though Latin America's processed and semi-manufactured commodity exports enjoy the advantages of non-discriminatory trade preferences in Australia, Canada, and Japan.

Though Latin America's overall trans-Pacific economic relations can be expected to expand substantially over the next decade, trade with some parts of the region will be more dynamic than with others. It is likely, for example, that Canada, Australia, and Japan, seeking new outlets for their manufactured exports, will provide the driving force for the expansion of trade, rather than the Latin American countries. Above all, Japan will be the most dynamic center of economic interchange with Latin America, rivaling the United States as the major trading partner with an increasing number of countries.

Already Japan has sharply increased its export of machinery and equipment to Brazil, Chile, and Peru, and taken industrial raw materials in exchange to balance the trade. Large Japanese-based international corporations are present in increasing numbers in Latin America as contractors for state-owned projects such as steel mills, oil refineries, and port facilities. Japan's special interest in these three countries has increased steadily, involving rather small outlays of Japanese capital, a more significant transfer of technology embodied in capital goods and technical assistance, and the import of newly exploited raw materials by Japan.

Canadian direct investment in the Pacific coast countries of Latin America is not large. Apart from the United States, Latin America as a whole represents the single largest area of Canadian private direct investment abroad. Although these Canadian investments are concentrated predominantly in public utilities, banking, and mining in the Caribbean and Central America, there are some significant investments in mining and related metal processing in the Andean countries of the Pacific coast.

As for Australia, private direct investment in Latin America is virtually non-existent. Australia, New Zealand, and Canada traditionally have been capital importing countries, but with the entry of Great Britain into the Common Market, they may be compelled to reorient their trade patterns and give trans-Pacific commercial relations with Latin America a higher priority.

Australia is rapidly forging closer economic links with the Latin American primary-commodity-exporting countries, through membership in various producer cartels. In April 1975, the government of Australia joined ten other major iron ore producers in establishing the Association of Iron Ore Producing and Exporting Countries (AIOPEC).[3] The purpose of the **AIOPEC** is to stabilize world iron export prices, encourage domestic processing, and exchange technical information. Canada refused to join because AIOPEC does not include consumer nations. Australia is also a member of the International Bauxite Association (IBA) and participates in an informal group of sugar producers that meet in London.

III. RELATIONS WITH JAPAN

Japan's economic relations with Latin America have expanded enormously in recent years, with annual export growth rates averaging nearly 30 percent since 1968. In fourteen years, Japanese exports to Latin America have expanded ninefold, climbing from $303 million in 1960 (when Japanese exports totalled $4 billion) to $2.8 billion in 1973 (when Japanese exports totalled $40 billion). Japanese exports to Latin America generally have grown as fast as Japanese world trade since 1960, although the growth rate has accelerated since the end of the 1960s. The Latin American market is still a marginal one for Japanese exporters, absorbing only 7.5 percent of total exports in 1973. From the Latin American vantage point, however, Japan has moved from the position of a relative insignificant supplier to become an important alternative to the United States and Western Europe. In 1960, Japan provided 3.5 percent of Latin American imports; in 1973, about 13 percent.

The Japanese export market has become increasingly important to the Latin American countries in the 1960s. Latin America's exports to Japan have been expanding faster than total Latin American exports during the decade. Japan's share in total Latin American exports rose from 2.0 percent in 1960 to 6.1 percent in 1970, but declined thereafter. From the Japanese viewpoint, however, imports from Latin America have been growing at a slower rate than total Japanese purchases. During the 1960s, Japan drew about 8.5 percent of its total imports from Latin America; by 1973, the share had dropped to 5.1 percent. The sharp fall that occurred after 1972 resulted from the abrupt rise in the value of Japan's oil imports, in large measure induced by OPEC pricing policy and revaluation of the yen.

Despite the recent slowdown in Japanese imports of Latin American goods (mainly metals, ores, crude materials, foodstuffs, and simple manufactures) the long-range potential for regional sales to Japan is enormous. The main Latin American suppliers are Brazil (foodstuffs, ores), Cuba (foodstuffs), Mexico (textiles), Chile (ores), Peru (ores), and Argentina (foodstuffs). In short, Japan is rapidly emerging as a major economic partner for an increasing number of Latin American countries, and a formidable competitor for North America and Western Europe.

Japanese direct investment in Latin America has risen dramatically from $380 million in 1967 to $1.8 billion in 1973 (see Table 1). In 1973, it accounted for 17.6 percent of Japan's total overseas direct investment of $10.3 billion. Compared to the magnitude of U.S. investment in Latin America—$18.5 billion in 1973—the level of Japanese investment is still low. It should be noted, however, that it is growing far more rapidly than American

TABLE 1
Japanese Overseas Investment,
By Region Of The World, 1973
(millions of U.S. dollars)

	1967	%	1973	%
North America	406	28.0	2,462	24.0
Latin America	380	26.2	1,811	17.6
Asia	310	21.4	2,391	23.3
Middle East	240	16.5	1,496	14.5
Europe	58	4.0	1,217	11.9
Africa	18	1.2	254	2.5
Oceania	39	2.7	640	6.2
	1,451	100.0	10,271	100.0

Source: **Ministry of International Trade and Industry, 1974 Report on Japanese Overseas Enterprises Activities,** Tokyo.

TABLE 2
**Comparison Of U.S. And Japanese Trade Turnover
And Investment In Latin America, 1965-1973**
(millions of U.S. dollars)

	Trade Turnover[a]		Direct Investment	
	1965	1973	1965	1973
United States	7,494	19,595	10,900	18,452
Japan	1,065.6	4,716	380[b]	1,811
Japan as Percent of U.S.	14.2	24.1	3.5	9.8

Source: IMF, **Direction of Trade**, annual issues, 1962-1966; U.S. Department of Commerce, **Survey of Current Business**, March 1975 and August 1974; and Ministry of International Trade and Industry, Tokyo.
a/ Trade turnover is equal to exports plus imports.
b/ 1967

or European investment (see Table 2). From the Japanese viewpoint, Latin America is receiving a declining share of Japan's total overseas investment, while the relative importance of Asia and Europe is growing. Japanese investors have given primary emphasis to Latin American manufacturing, allocating nearly 60 percent of total investment resources to this sector and only 10 percent to mining. Japanese interest in resource development projects, however, is clearly on the rise—particularly in Brazil, Chile, Peru, and Venezuela. Japanese joint ventures and official economic aid will be directed to the development of Latin American mining and agriculture in the future.

Brazil received over half of the total Japanese direct investment in the region, amounting to over $1 billion in early 1974. Japan's investments in Brazil include the USIMINAS steel works, as well as large-scale projects in shipbuilding, automobiles, and textiles. Japanese capital provides an important share of total foreign capital in Brazil's shipbuilding (81 percent), steel (44 percent), timber industries (31 percent), with significant amounts in textiles, machinery, and finance. Expansion is planned in shipbuilding, steel, chemical fertilizers, and aluminum fabrication. A joint Brazilian-Japanese aluminum plant, the world's largest, to be constructed at a cost of $2.4 billion, was approved by both governments in 1974.

With the rapid expansion of its overseas direct investments, Japan has become increasingly aware of the potential for serious friction with recipient countries, particularly in Southeast Asia (Thailand and Indonesia), where local nationalists strongly resent the dominant Japanese investment position in many industries and the aggressive Japanese business behavior. At present, Japanese investors have an enviable degree of acceptability in Argentina, Brazil, Mexico, Peru, and other countries of the region, due in large measure to their low investment profile and still unobtrusive presence. Furthermore, the Japanese do not have a history of conflictive economic relations with Latin America. However, the continuation of good relations with the Latin American countries may require much greater Japanese government efforts, particularly as Japan's investments in certain countries and economic sectors can be expected to assume a larger dimension over the next decade.

Japan has the second largest development aid program in the world after the United States. Nevertheless, less than 5 percent of Japanese official bilateral aid went to Latin America in 1973 (compared to 90 percent to Asia), which was still a considerable improvement over prior years. Latin America, however, received a far higher share (46 percent or about $2.7 billion) of total Japanese resource flows (including bilateral and multilateral aid, export credits, private portfolio and direct investment), which amounted to $5.8 billion in 1973. Measured by total Japanese resource flows, Latin America is beginning to rival Asia.

The Japanese government considers the Latin American countries too developed, in general, to receive large-scale bilateral aid, and prefers to see private investment playing the predominant role in Japanese-Latin American economic relations. The Japanese authorities seem to be aware, however, that the maintenance of harmonious economic relations with Latin America (as well as with other regions) may require an increase in bilateral development aid, and a more generous treatment of Latin American exports under Japan's preferential tariff scheme of 1971.

IV. RELATIONS WITH CANADA

The bulk of Canada's political and economic interests within the Western Hemisphere (the United States apart) have been concentrated on the independent states and territories of the British Commonwealth Caribbean. These interests have been the natural outgrowth of the eighteenth and nineteenth century commercial association between British North America and the British West Indies. At present, Canada has substantial trade and investment relations with Jamaica, Trinidad-Tobago, the Bahamas, Barbados, and to a declining extent, Guyana. Canada has substantial investments in banking, real estate, life insurance, manufacturing, and tourism.

Until recently, Canada's deep-seated mistrust of American expansion and power in the hemisphere has inhibited Canadian involvement in Latin America and the inter-American system. Furthermore, the development of increasingly complex Canadian-American economic and financial relations has deterred Canada from joining inter-American organizations, such as the OAS, which might bring Canada into direct conflict with the United States to the detriment of more important bilateral interests.

Nevertheless, Canada is beginning to move cautiously towards a deeper involvement in inter-American affairs. An important step was taken in May 1972 when Canada became a member of the Inter-American Development Bank. Canada has appointed an official observer to the OAS, but still has not become a full member. Public opinion in Canada reflects the persistence of a sense of alienation from Spanish and Portuguese America, its problems and accomplishments. Prime Minister Pierre Trudeau's foreign policy is attempting to overcome this sense of remoteness by stressing Canada's hemispheric interests and downgrading her NATO military role.

In the 1970s, the Canadian private and public sectors have made a substantial effort to expand commercial relations with the Latin American countries as part of Prime Minister Trudeau's "Third Option" trade policy—the diversification of trade relations outside Canada's traditional American and British markets. In 1974, Canada's exports to the Western Hemisphere (excluding the United States) reached $1.4 billion, up sharply from $862 million the previous year. In relation to Canada's 1974 exports to the United States of $20.6 billion, this is not a large volume of trade. Nevertheless, the Latin American market is no longer insignificant. And, as the 1970 *Foreign Policy White Paper* emphasized, trade expansion is a major goal of Canada's international relations.

In Latin America, Canada's four major trading partners are Cuba, Brazil, Mexico, and Venezuela. The Canadian government hopes to vastly expand its trade with Brazil over the next decade. Venezuela, owing to considerable competition from the United States, presents a more difficult problem for Canadian businessmen seeking trade and investment opportunities there. Special opportunities do exist, however, in those fields in which Canadians claim superiority, such as pulp and paper supply, hydro-power technology, and transport equipment. The Mexican State Railways, for example, recently purchased a $200 million package of railway cars, steel rails, and shop modernization from a consortium of Canadian firms.

Cuba is rapidly emerging as one of Canada's more important trading partners. In March 1975, the Canadian government announced an agreement to finance a $40 million fish processing plant in Havana, and to extend a $100 million commercial credit to Cuba. By 1980, the Canadian government expects exports to Cuba to rise to $400 million, up from $142 million in 1974. Cuba is not only viewed as an increasingly important outlet for its goods and services but Canadian businessmen hope to be able to preempt the lion's share of the Cuban market before U.S.-Cuban commercial relations are reestablished. It is doubtful, however, that Canada will be able to sustain a special position in the Cuban market for very long. Stiff U.S. competition will likely be felt not long after U.S.-Cuban relations are normalized.

While Canadian investment is still largely concentrated in the Commonwealth Caribbean, a process of diversification has been underway in recent years. Canada has a major investment in the Dominican Republic in Falconbrige Dominicana S.A. (nickel mining) and in Brazil in Brascan Limited (a diversified holding company). Brascan is Brazil's second largest foreign-owned corporation, and has expanded from public utility services into food processing, development banking, transport equipment manufacture, and real estate investment.

During the 1970s, Canadian-owned banks and industries have become the target of the kind of nationalist hostility customarily reserved for U.S. private enterprise in Latin America. In 1971, the Canadian-owned Demarara Bauxite Company (a subsidiary of the Aluminum Company of Canada—ALCAN), with assets valued at $150 million, was nationalized by the government of Guyana. This substantially reduced total Canadian investment in the Caribbean, which currently amounts to about $500 million, according to Canadian government estimates. The worst reaction to "Canadian imperialism" occurred in Trinidad-Tobago in 1970 when anti-Canadian riots were organized by West Indian nationalists.

Various governments in the region, such as those of Jamaica, Trinidad-Tobago, Guyana, and the Bahamas, are taking increasingly restrictive measures against Canadian and other private investment. During 1974, ALCAN and several U.S. companies were required to pay a new levy on bauxite production which sharply increased Jamaica's total revenue from an annual rate of $30 million in 1973 to $165 million in subsequent years. In January 1975, the U.S.-owned subsidiary of the Reynolds Aluminum Company, with book value of $15.5 million, was taken over, bringing Guyana's aluminum industry entirely under government ownership and control.

Economic relations with Latin America have been slow to develop because of Canada's traditional orientation toward Britain, the Commonwealth, and the United States. As a large net capital-importing country with attractive domestic investment opportunities, Canadians have been more inward-looking and less interested in expanding overseas than the Americans. But this is now changing. Trade expansion and development assistance has become an important aspect of Canada's hemispheric policy. Although Canada's dominance in the financial sector in the British Commonwealth Caribbean has created problems for its investments there, Canadian investments outside the English-speaking Caribbean are still well-received and prospects for closer Canadian-Latin American trade relations appear to be good.

V. RELATIONS WITH WESTERN EUROPE

With the exception of Spain, Western Europe seems to be only dimly aware of Latin America and relations with the region do not rank highly on the list of European political or economic priorities. Furthermore, Western Europe's commercial interest in Latin America is declining. In 1950, 8.5 percent of European exports went to Latin America; by 1960 this ratio had fallen to 6 percent; and in 1973 it was only 3.3 percent. From the Latin American point of view, however, Western Europe is an important market absorbing more than 30 percent of its exports and supplying about 30 percent of its imports, including much of the capital equipment essential to industrial growth. Thus, Latin American-Western European commercial relations are marked by a strong asymmetry. While Latin America is peripheral to European interests, the Latin American is deeply interested in its economic relations with Western Europe.

The Western European countries maintain an official optimism concerning trade with Latin America, but there is little substance to it in the light of hard economic realities. The traditional role assigned to Latin America by Western Europe of providing raw materials in exchange for manufactures is no longer satisfactory to Latin America nor in conformity with recent trends in Latin American trade. The most dynamic sector of Latin American exports over the decade of the 1960s was manufactured products.

And many of these manufactures and semi-manufactures are in direct competition with some parts of the European industrial structure.

Europe shows little concern for the impact of its trade and agricultural policies on Latin American development. Under the European Economic Community's (EEC) Common Agricultural Policy (CAP), Latin American interests have not been given the serious consideration they merit. Argentina, Uruguay, and Brazil, as well as other Latin American countries, produce and export temperate agricultural products that are highly protected by the CAP. When European farms face difficulty, the CAP forces the adjustment burden to fall as much as possible on competing exporters, including Latin America.

The EEC's preferential trade agreements established with its Associate Members in the early sixties have clearly hurt Latin American exports. Special tariff preferences have been given to a large number of African states, former colonies of France, Belgium, and Italy, whose tropical agricultural products (such as cocoa, coffee, and sugar) are directly competitive with those exported from the tropical Caribbean and South America.

More recently, in February 1975, the EEC signed the Lomé Agreement which discriminates seriously against the tropical exporting countries of the Caribbean (except Jamaica, Trinidad and Tobago, and Barbados), and Central and South America. The Lomé Agreement provides duty free access for a wide range of tropical exports (with the exception of sugar) from the 46 countries of Africa, the Caribbean, and the Pacific (the so-called ACP countries). No reciprocity, in the form of reverse preferences, has been given to the EEC by the ACP members.[4]

Most of the anticipated gains of the EEC's generalized system of preferences, which was set up to encourage the manufactured exports of the less developed countries, have yet to be realized. The non-preferential trade agreements signed between the EEC and Argentina, Brazil, and Uruguay have little economic meaning or impact. Furthermore, the trade credits provided by Europe to facilitate trade with Latin America have primarily benefited European exports and often carry burdensome terms for Latin American imports. It is clear, therefore, that until Latin America becomes a priority interest in the economic councils of Western Europe, little improvement in Latin America's overall position in the Western European market can be expected.

The Latin American countries look to Western Europe as a counterweight to the influence of the United States. They would like European support for the reorganization of the world economy along more favorable lines leading to improved terms of trade for exports of raw materials, increased access to world markets for manufactured exports, and expanded local ownership of the means of production. Thus far Europe has not given serious support to these initiatives, but there is the hope that a new GATT negotiation, which will include Latin America as well as other LDCs as full participating members, could provide a mechanism for resolving some of these problems.

Traditionally, most Latin American countries have considered themselves too dependent on others, but they are generally less dependent on the international economy than many regions of the world. For example, the ratios of exports and imports to GNP are lower in Latin America than those that are typically found in Europe. The share of foreign ownership of natural resources is no higher in Latin America than in Canada and Australia, nor greater in the manufacturing sector than in Canada, the United Kingdom, and West Germany. Furthermore, the Latin American countries are also less dependent on world capital markets than either Britain or Italy. They receive less concessionary aid than other less developed countries because, compared to Africa and Asia, Latin America is considered a more advanced area. In addition, the labor markets of most Latin American countries have been less affected by immigration and emigration of workers than is the case of Europe.

From the Latin American viewpoint, however, their current dependency on political and economic forces beyond their control is excessive. The traditional products that Latin America exports have prices determined in world markets over which they have little control. Moreover, these prices declined steadily from peaks in the early 1950s and caused a deterioration in the terms of trade which Latin America felt helpless to reverse. Foreign firms with direct investments in Latin America tend to dominate the industries in which they operate and are the most dynamic and promising industries for the future. Few Latin American domestic firms have a countervailing power to protect local interests. Extensive state regulation and control of foreign investment has been introduced, however, in most Latin American countries, which insures that the national interest is protected.

With the end of World War II, many Latin American countries adopted an import replacing development strategy and these policies, aimed at reducing dependence, have met with mixed success. Tax and credit policies directed to stimulate investment in industry led to inequitable tax burdens and fragmented capital markets. High tariffs and quotas on imports protected many undersized and inefficient producers. Foreign exchange controls and multiple exchange rate systems yielded overvalued currencies which discouraged exports. This conscious effort to reduce dependency succeeded since Latin America's share of world trade fell from 11 percent in 1950 to 7.8 percent in 1960 to 5.6 percent in 1970 to 4.5 percent in 1973.

Unfortunately, these policies created economic inefficiency and misallocation of resources in many countries. While successful in stimulating industrial growth, they failed to reduce Latin America's dependence on world markets. The Latin American countries continued to export raw materials and food products that were subject to world market fluctuations. Yet, it was these exports that provided the foreign exchange earnings needed to finance the import of machinery and equipment essential for domestic economic growth.

Latin American industrial growth was also limited by the size of domestic markets. Foreign firms were attracted by the high level of protection to make direct investments to serve the local markets and these firms were often able to outperform locally-owned firms. The formation of customs unions and free trade areas followed as the next phase of Latin American economic policy, but the Latin American Free Trade Association failed to live up to expectations. A long-range commitment requiring short-term losses to bring about future gains was never made. In several Latin American nations, exchange rate reforms and specific export stimulants have been tried and in some cases have been very successful in boosting trade and accelerating growth. These policies have not helped, however, to correct the inequalities of income distribution and excessive urban concentration that have accompanied growth in Latin America.

The nations of Latin America seek certain specific objectives from a reorganized world economy:

(1) They continue to strive for an improvement in the terms of trade for the raw materials they export.

(2) They seek improved access in the markets of the industrial countries for their manufactured exports.

(3) They seek help in establishing more advanced industries with substantial Latin American ownership.

(4) With regard to European policy, the Latin American countries want improvements in the EEC generalized tariff preference scheme, improvements that could come through fewer exceptions, more liberalized quotas, and less stringent escape clauses.

(5) They also seek to negotiate commodity agreements that would include commercial and industrial cooperation and promote capital investment and the transfer of technological and scientific knowledge. Such agreements need not conflict with the EEC's obligations to other nations and could provide real benefits to the nations of Latin America.

Western Europe clearly could do far more to assist Latin American development, but from the European viewpoint there is more to be gained from economic relations with Asia, Africa, and other developing regions. In light of this continuing asymmetry of economic position, it is not realistic to anticipate any imminent, fundamental change in Western Europe's calculated indifference towards Latin America.

VI. RELATIONS WITH THE SOVIET UNION, EASTERN EUROPE, AND CHINA

During the 1960s, and particularly since the end of the decade, an increasing number of Caribbean and South American states have established diplomatic and commercial relations with the Soviet Union, Eastern Europe, and China.[5] The major economic partners of the socialist states are the larger Latin American states, Argentina and Brazil, and to a lesser extent Peru and Colombia. Mexico has not yet established any significant trade relations with the socialist countries, although trade and economic missions were sent to Russia, China, and the Eastern European countries in the mid-seventies.

Various factors have contributed to Latin America's growing interest in economic relations with the socialist states: the widespread desire to diversify export markets and obtain new sources of capital and technology; the protectionist trend in the United States that has forced certain Latin American exporters to seek markets elsewhere; the difficulty of competing in the EEC with Asian and African countries receiving preferential treatment; the balance of payments pressures resulting from higher oil prices; and the nationalistic trend in the region which has generated interest in relations with the socialist states as a demonstration of "independence" from the United States.

From the viewpoint of the Soviet Union and Eastern European countries, Latin America is a marginal trading area. Commercial interchange is growing in absolute terms, but is declining in relative importance to the Soviet bloc. Latin America's share of total Council for Mutual Economic Assistance (CMEA) trade is diminishing because of the more rapid growth of trade of the latter with the industrialized world. Nevertheless, an effort is being made by the Soviet Union and the Eastern European countries to broaden trade relations with Latin America and to create "mechanisms of cooperation" that will lend a more regular and stable character to economic relations with the region.

Despite the desire on both sides to strengthen economic relations, there are substantial difficulties that must be overcome. Foremost among them is the fact that the Soviet Union, China, and the Eastern European countries have a persistently unfavorable trade balance with Latin America, which inhibits the further expansion of commercial interchange. In general, Latin America exports its traditional primary commodities (sugar, coffee, cacao, hides, fruit, tin) to the socialist countries, although some exports of semi-manufactured and manufactured goods have begun. The Soviet Union and Eastern European countries mainly export machinery and equipment to Latin America, which face the strong competition of the region's major suppliers: the United States, the EEC countries, and Japan.

The trade relations of Russia and the individual Eastern European countries with Latin America (Cuba excluded) are of minor significance. Soviet imports from Latin America reached only $284 million in 1973. They nevertheless, have been rising in absolute figures in recent years, and can be expected to expand slowly in the future. Soviet exports reached a peak of $66 million in 1966 and have generally declined since then. Soviet trade is heavily concentrated on Argentina, Brazil, and more recently Peru, which together accounted for almost 90 percent of total Soviet trade in 1973. Peru has become an increasingly important trading partner in recent years.

The Eastern European socialist countries have made independent efforts to establish trade relations with Latin America. To a greater extent than the Soviet Union, the Eastern European countries have a need for some of the raw materials exported by Latin America. Eastern European trade turnover with Latin America reached $434 million in 1972, compared with a Soviet trade turnover of $179 million (see Table 3). This trade has been steadily expanding and has demonstrated a momentum lacking in Soviet trade relations. Brazil, Argentina, Peru, and Colombia account for about 90 percent of the East European trade turnover in the hemisphere in recent years. The East Europeans have begun to explore mixed state enterprises financed by local and socialist state capital as a technique for generating additional exports to Latin America. In 1973, the state mining companies of Romania (GEOMIN) and Peru (MINEROPERU) established a jointly-owned state mining enterprise to exploit the Atamina copper deposits.

Soviet economic aid to Latin America (again excluding Cuba) was negligible throughout the 1960s, but has been rising in the 1970s as new opportunities presented themselves. About two-thirds of all Soviet aid has gone to countries close to the Soviet borders, and Latin America ranks last in order of priority among recipient regions of the world. Despite the rise in Soviet economic aid, it is still characterized by its small scale and instability. During the 1966-1973 period, Chile was the largest aid recipient, receiving $260.5 million under the Allende regime, and accounting for over half of total Soviet aid to Latin America. Brazil received a $85 million credit in 1966, making it the second most important aid recipient in the region. In 1973, however, no Soviet aid was authorized for any Latin American country.

During the last ten years, East European countries have provided little economic aid to Latin America. Most of what there was has been delivered to two countries: Peru and Chile. By 1973, East European aid had fallen to $5 million from a high point in 1970 of $174 million.

Chinese economic activity in Latin America is still modest. Peking's exports are negligible, fluctuating within the narrow range of $4-8 million in the 1968-1972 period. But Chinese imports from Latin America have risen rapidly, from less than $1 million in 1968 to $191 million in 1972. Chile, Brazil, and Peru

TABLE 3
Soviet Union, Eastern European, And
Chinese Trade With Latin America, 1968-1972
(millions of U.S. dollars)

	1968			1970			1972		
	Exports	Imports	Turnover	Exports	Imports	Turnover	Exports	Imports	Turnover
Soviet Union	25.3	68.3	93.6	13.0	62.0	75.0	31.7	147.2	178.9
Eastern Europe	127.8	189.5	317.3	137.6	250.9	388.5	144.1	290.0	434.1
China	6.8	0.6	7.4	3.9	3.8	7.7	7.1	190.9	198.0
Total	159.9	258.4	418.3	154.5	316.7	471.2	182.9	628.1	811.0

Source: U.S. Department of State, Bureau of Intelligence and Research, Communist States and Developing Countries: AID and Trade, 1969, 1971, and 1973.

are the main Chinese trading partners, accounting for about 95 percent of total Chinese trade with Latin America in 1972. Trading activity, however, despite its advances, is still highly unstable.

Peking's only economic aid to Latin America, a total of $133 million, was authorized in 1971 and 1972. In 1971, aid was given to Peru and Chile and in 1972 to Chile and Guyana. No aid was authorized for Latin America in 1973. Within Peking's foreign aid priorities, Latin America has the lowest position in the Third World, trailing behind the nations of Africa, South Asia, and the Middle East.

In 1974, total Latin American exports to the Soviet Union, Eastern Europe, and China exceeded $1 billion. Socialist trade with Latin America can be expected to continue to grow in absolute terms, offering another useful outlet for the exports of the Latin American countries. Nevertheless, its relative importance to Latin America as a trading area is not likely to change significantly.

Socialist bloc-Latin American trade will continue to be limited for some time to come by the sluggishness of the communist state trading bureaucracies, the rigidity of the national five-year plans which restrict the expansion of the foreign sector, the unsuitability or high price of socialist manufactured goods, unfamiliarity with the Latin American market, and inefficiency in providing spare parts, components, and after-sales servicing. Some of these obstacles are slowly being overcome, but a large-scale expansion of trade between the Soviet Union, Eastern Europe, China, and Latin America does not appear likely for the foreseeable future.

The economic aid program will remain an important element of Soviet and Chinese policy towards the Third World, but a large-scale commitment to Latin America, even to a friendly socialist government such as Allende's Communist-Socialist coalition in Chile, is highly unlikely. Both Moscow and Peking refused to provide the massive economic aid that the Allende government sought, and needed to survive. Moscow will continue to provide economic aid to Latin American countries on a highly selective basis, when the political situation warrants it. Moscow's economic (and military) aid program remains one of the few available instruments for expanding Soviet influence in Latin America, weakening U.S.-Latin American ties, and countering Chinese influence.

VII. RELATIONS WITH THE THIRD WORLD

Historically, the political and economic relations between the developing countries of Asia, Africa, the Middle East, and Latin America have been weak and sporadic. For a variety of reasons—partly geographical and traditional, reflecting European colonial and post-colonial ties; and partly structural, reflecting comparative advantage in commodity production—Latin America's trading relations have concentrated on North America and Western Europe.

Over the past two decades, and particularly in recent years, this traditional pattern of relations has begun to change. Political and economic interactions between Latin America and the rest of the developing world (that is, south-south relations) have been intensified. Financial, commercial, investment, and technical ties have been established where, in general, none existed before. In the mid-seventies, the impact of the oil crisis in Latin America and the rise of petrodollar surpluses in the oil-exporting Middle East countries have had an immediate impact on Latin American-Middle Eastern relations.

Brazil has taken the lead in establishing financial, trade, and investment ties with a number of Middle East oil-exporting nations. It has established oil-exploration agreements with Egypt, Iraq, and Libya. It is planning to participate in a $500 million iron and steel complex in Saudi Arabia, exchanging Brazilian iron ore for Saudi oil. Trade agreements have also been signed with Kuwait under which Brazil will supply manufactured goods and rice for oil. As the largest Latin American oil-importing state (net imports of $2.7 billion in 1974 compared to $588 million for Argentina), Brazil is understandably concerned about expanding and securing its overseas sources of supply.

Most of Argentina's trade and investment ties in the Middle East have been with Libya. The Qadaffi regime, which claims to be a great admirer of Peron and Peron's "Third Position" (neither capitalism nor communism), has entered into six commercial agreements with Argentina (sugar and cereals for oil) and extended a $200 million commercial credit payable in Argentine raw materials. In addition, Argentina has signed a nuclear research agreement with Libya, and has agreed to barter conventional weapons for Libyan oil and investments. But Argentina is largely self-sufficient in oil production, and therefore under less pressure than Brazil to establish diversified economic ties with the Middle East oil exporting nations.

A growing number of Latin American republics consider themselves, in some respects at least, as part of the so-called non-aligned Third World, of which Moscow's Cuban client was a founding member. Third World efforts to alter the international economic system in its favor through confrontation tactics have attracted the support of some Latin American countries—notably Mexico, Venezuela, Argentina, Peru, and Guyana.

In the economic sphere, new commodity arrangements among Latin American and other Third World producers have been established for oil (OPEC), copper (CIPEC), bauxite (IBA), and some other commodities. Latin American countries have also been actively cooperating with other Third World countries in the United Nations, UNCTAD, the so-called Non-Aligned Group, and elsewhere. These interactions have helped to define a Third World ideology with a strong anti-Western bias.

Still, the direct interactions involving trade, investment, and aid flows between individual Latin American countries and the other developing regions are not very intensive. Latin American countries have cooperative and conflictive relations not only among themselves, but also with other developing countries. At the world level, the Latin American countries have increasingly used the proliferating international organizations (United Nations, UNCTAD, UNIDO) and less formally organized groups such as the so-called Non-Aligned Group, to conduct their international relations, to bring pressure to bear on the industrial countries, and to define their common interests.

Latin American exports to the Third World (excluding intra-Latin American trade) have been rising steadily in the post-World War II period. But their relative importance, measured as a share of total Latin American exports, has been declining and is now below 10 percent. For some countries, like Brazil, which is heavily dependent on oil imports (from the Middle East and Africa) this general picture of the declining importance of Latin American-Third World trade may not be quite accurate. Meanwhile, intra-Latin American trade is far more dynamic, raising the share of intra-trade to total Latin American trade over the past fifteen years.

The relative unimportance of Latin American trade with the other developing regions stems from the competitive nature of their economies. But as more Latin American countries shift from semi-industrial to industrial economies, the prospects for trade with Africa, Asia, and Middle East will tend to improve, as suggested by the case of Brazil.

There are wide areas of common interest between the Latin American and other Third World countries that do improve the prospects for Third World cohesion and cooperation. This is especially true for economic issues such as the barriers to manufactured exports imposed by the industrial world and the treatment of multinational enterprises. On the other hand, serious differences exist between the Third World countries concerning trade preferences, negotiating strategy, regulation of foreign investment, and the unequal distribution of benefits from commodity cartels. With respect to trade preferences, the most common divisions are between EEC associated developing countries and non-EEC associated developing countries, especially Latin America; and between more and less developed countries of the Third World.

Therefore, while economic interactions between Latin America and the Third World have been on the rise, they are still far less important for Latin American development than relations with the industrial countries of North America, Western Europe, and Japan. Latin American-Third World trade flows, except for oil, are experiencing a modest rise in absolute terms but are of negligible relative importance.

VIII. FOOD PRODUCTION

Before World War II, Latin America was the most important food exporting region (mainly grains and cereals) in the world. Over the past quarter century, however, regional food production has lagged behind local consumption requirements which has resulted in the inevitable concomitant decline in net food exports. In 1934-1938, Latin America was exporting (net) 9 million metric tons of wheat (mainly from Argentina) but by 1973 the region was importing 5.5 million metric tons (see Table 4). In 1973, Latin America was also a net importer of rice (400 thousand metric tons), meat (1 million metric tons), and other food commodities such as sugar, coffee, cocoa, bananas, and other fruits and vegetables.[6] Viewed in the context of world food production, Latin America is now barely able to maintain self-sufficiency as a food-producing region.

Why has this situation come to pass in a region considered by some agricultural experts as capable of feeding a population twice its present size? The slow growth of Latin America's agricultural production can be attributed largely to the post-war drive for industrialization that led most governments to discriminate severely against the farmer and in favor of urban industry and labor. Low farm prices, heavy export taxes, discriminatory exchange rates, high priced locally produced inputs, marketing inefficiencies, credit scarcities, inadequate extension services and problem-oriented research, and poor official policy planning—all these factors played a part in reducing the incentive to produce and export agricultural products.

Latin America has more unused land available for crop production than the rest of the world combined. At present, only about 16 percent of the region's available agricultural land is cultivated leaving over 400 million hectares of land potentially available for cultivation. Over the next decade, Latin American agriculture should continue to expand at about the 3 percent per annum necessary to keep pace with population growth and provide a modest surplus, but Brazil, Argentina, and many other countries have the potential to greatly increase their agricultural production.

Argentina's long-term decline in the world food markets is attributable mainly to discriminatory price controls, production and export taxes, and other domestic policies that have severely distorted incentives to produce and consume food. Argentine food prices are among the lowest in the world, and grain farmers receive less than half the world price for their exports. On the other hand, Brazilian farmers have received strong economic

TABLE 4
Pattern Of World Grain Trade
(millions of metric tons)

	1934-1938	1948-1952	1960	1969-1971	1973E
North America	+ 5	+23	+39	+54	+91
Latin America	+ 9	+ 1	0	+ 3	− 2
Western Europe	−24	−22	−25	−22	−20
Eastern Europe and Russia	+ 5	—	0	− 3	−12
Africa	+ 1	0	− 2	− 3	− 6
Asia	+ 2	− 6	−17	−31	−60
Australia and New Zealand	+ 3	+ 3	+ 6	+11	+ 9

Note: Plus sign denotes net exports and minus sign denotes net imports. Grains include wheat and coarse grains.
E = Estimate.
Source: U.N. Food and Agriculture Organization and the U.S. Department of Agriculture.

incentives, and agricultural exports have risen from $1.2 billion in 1963 to $2.7 billion in 1972, and continue to grow. Large sectors of Brazilian agriculture are being modernized, and producers are responding to changes in the international markets. Thus, Argentina and Brazil point up the rich potential and mixed achievements of food production in Latin America.

Agrarian reform continues to be a key issue in many Latin American countries. The problems of raising agricultural productivity, expanding output, and improving the living standards of the *campesino* persist even in countries like Mexico, Bolivia, Peru, and Chile where substantial land redistribution has taken place. The impact of agrarian reform on agricultural output, productivity, exports, and consumption depends essentially on the nature and scope of the reforms, the extent to which official policy provides a framework of economic incentives for producers, and the availability of credit, technical, marketing, and other assistance to the reformed sector.

The great diversity of objectives and ideas about what constitutes agrarian reform in Latin America are often highly colored by ideological considerations. Nevertheless, many proponents of agrarian reform agree that it should transform unjust systems of land tenure, improve the welfare of the peasant, and bring about a redistribution of domestic income and political power.

The principle of comparative advantage suggests that Latin America should be a large net food-exporting region. In the 1950s, however, the Latin American countries decided to pursue income growth through industrialization. The relative decline of Latin American agriculture was the unintended result of that choice. In the seventies, there is a much greater awareness in Latin America of the importance of the agricultural sector for rapid and balanced economic growth. The Latin American region could again become a major exporter of food if governments provide an adequate framework of economic incentives and assistance to the agricultural producer.

IX. MINERAL RAW MATERIALS PRODUCTION

Since colonial times, the production and export of mineral (and agricultural) raw materials has played a major part in the incorporation of Latin America into the world economy. Mineral exporting countries have become closely linked—financially, commercially, and technologically—to the major industrial consuming centers in North America and Western Europe. Because of its large capital requirements, mineral development has attracted a large flow of foreign investment to the mineral-rich countries like Bolivia, Chile, Peru, and Venezuela. While the pattern of ownership and control of the extractive sector in Latin America is changing, (with state-owned mining enterprise the predominant emerging form), the American, British, and other European firms that originally set up the resource industries continue to play an important role in providing capital, technology, management, and world marketing facilities.

Mineral raw materials development has played a central role in the economies of the Latin American nations, with copper and iron ore the most important in recent years. Before 1930, the dependence on raw materials exports was unchallenged. During the 1960s, the acceleration of import substituting industrialization, the increased use of mineral raw materials in local production, and the expansion of manufactured exports have

Aside from petroleum, and perhaps bauxite, producer cartels are not likely to be successful in the raw materials markets. Some commodity price stabilization may be possible, but it is unlikely to result in notably larger returns to producers. Copper and iron ore are expected to play a larger role in the world economy, but for the Latin American region primary commodity exports will continue to decrease in importance as manufactured exports expand.

X. LATIN AMERICA AS WORLD OIL SUPPLIER

Latin America has been a major source of world production and export of oil since the early part of the twentieth century. Production outpaced consumption in the region until the mid-1960s when net exports reached a peak of 2.7 million barrels a day in 1964. Since that time, however, Latin America has become a declining net oil exporting region as regional consumption has been rising faster than production.

For the purpose of analyzing the regional petroleum balance, the Latin American countries can be divided into three categories: net oil exporters (Bolivia, Ecuador, Trinidad-Tobago, Venezuela, and Mexico); countries presently or potentially self-sufficient (Colombia, Argentina, Peru); and net oil importers (Brazil, Chile, Cuba, Dominican Republic, Haiti, Jamaica, Central America, Paraguay, and Uruguay).

In 1975, Mexico became a net oil exporter and Peru may achieve that status by the late seventies or early eighties as its Amazon basin reserves are developed. Ecuador and Mexico are the only other countries that have a significant export potential in the near and medium term. It is unlikely that Colombia and Argentina will become significant oil exporting countries or that the other net oil importing countries will be come self-sufficient in the near future. The balance of payments and economic growth performance of the net oil-importing countries have suffered considerably from the fourfold OPEC-induced rise in oil prices in 1972-1974. These countries compete with the other oil-importing countries of the world, including the United States, for world oil supplies.

Although deliberately reducing production in the interest of conservation, Venezuela can be expected to maintain its position as Latin America's most important oil exporting country at least through the 1980s. It accounts for about 92 percent of the total value of regional exports (1974). Ecuador, Mexico, and Trinidad-Tobago lag far behind, together accounting for only 8 percent of total gross exports.

The United States is the major market for regional exports, taking about 50 percent of Venezuela's exports (1974) and about 70 percent of all Caribbean exports, together totalling about 2,540,000 barrels a day in 1973. Over half of Latin American oil exports are refined petroleum products, much of which goes to the United States in the form of residual fuel oil.

Most of Latin America's oil has been discovered, produced, and marketed by private foreign oil companies—for the most part U.S. owned. The share of the region's oil produced by private firms has been declining sharply since the early sixties, as state-owned oil enterprises have increasingly taken over private concessions and expanded production in new areas. Foreign oil companies have been expropriated in Peru (the International Petroleum Company was taken over in 1968), and Venezuela (oil company concessions expired in 1975), and state petroleum companies have a monopoly on production in Brazil, Chile, Mexico, Argentina, and Bolivia.

Traditional concession arrangements still exist in some countries (notably Trinidad-Tobago, Ecuador, and Bolivia), but government policy in Latin America is clearly shifting away from concessions and towards service contracts to expand output and reserves. Joint venture companies formed by state oil companies and private firms are also under consideration by many countries. This revolution in relations between foreign oil companies and Latin American governments is part of a global movement to restrict the companies' power and profits and to increase the government's monpoly rents and power of decision. The end result of this process will be to confine the private oil companies to sellers of services, which does not necessarily imply the termination of private-sector oil exploration and development. The large number of firms working in Peru, Ecuador, and Bolivia confirm that service contracts can still be profitable for privately-owned oil companies.

The total proved reserves of crude oil in Latin America (1974) are approximately 40 billion barrels—some 15 billion (37.0 percent) in Venezuela, 13.6 billion (33.5 percent) in Mexico, and 2.5 billion (6.6 percent) in Ecuador, Trinidad-Tobago, and Peru, respectively. According to preliminary reports, Mexico has very substantial newly proved reserves, but no authoritative official estimates are available yet. Venezuela's share of regional reserves has declined steadily over the past decade, while Mexico and Ecuador have emerged with the region's second and third largest reserves, respectively (see Table 5).

Far more oil may ultimately be recovered than is indicated in the figures of proved oil reserves. Venezuela's oil resources alone are estimated at 150 billion barrels, ten times the proved reserves,

TABLE 5
Latin American Proved Reserves Of Oil
(millions of barrels)

Country	January 1975 Oil	Percent
Argentina	2,346	5.8
Barbados	25	a/
Bolivia	250	.6
Brazil	775	1.9
Chile	200	.5
Colombia	900	2.2
Ecuador	2,500	6.2
Mexico	13,582	33.5
Peru	2,500	6.2
Trinidad-Tobago	2,500	6.2
Venezuela	15,000	36.9
Total	40,578	100.0

Source: **The Gas & Oil Journal**, Tulsa, Oklahoma, December 30, 1974
a/ less than one percent.

excluding the heavy oil belt. Additional proved reserves are most likely to be found in the southern zone of Lake Maracaibo, the Gulf of Venezuela, and the Gulf of Vela. Furthermore, the heavy oil belt along the Orinoco River is estimated (none too precisely) to have 700-800 billions of barrels of oil capable of recovery with present heavy oil technology. The Venezuelan Government reputedly has assigned an initial $1.5 billion to extract oil from this belt, with the aim of reaching an output of 300,000 barrels a day by 1981 and 500,000 barrels by 1985.

Another area likely to yield substantial new oil supplies in the near future is the Upper Amazon Basin of Peru, Ecuador, and Brazil, and the adjacent Beni area in Bolivia, which is now being actively explored by foreign oil companies. Over the next decade or two, Latin America's role as a net oil exporting region will continue to decline and its importance as a supplier to the United States will steadily diminish.

XI. CONVENTIONAL ARMS TRANSFER

The transfer of conventional arms from the developed weapons-producing nations to Latin America over the past decade has been modest in comparison with all other world regions (see Table 6). Latin American arms imports have never reached $500 million in any single year, but there has been a slight increase in the value of imports in the 1970s. Latin America's share of world total arms imports has risen slightly from 4.4 percent in 1963 to 5.1 percent in 1973. The major arms-importing countries over the past decade have been Argentina, Brazil, Cuba, Peru, and Venezuela.

Latin America's arms expenditures also have been modest on a world-scale. Military expenditures as a share of GNP in Latin America has remained basically constant during the decade (about 2 percent or below) which is the lowest of any geographic region. Latin America's per capita military expenditures have never exceeded $12 a year, and in 1973 was $8 a year compared with the world average of $62 and the developed countries average of $206. The average per capita cost of arms purchases by the Latin American countries during the decade (subtracting known grant aid) was as follows: Over $35-Cuba; $20-Peru and Venezuela; $10 to $15-Chile and Argentina. All the other Latin American nations, including Brazil, spent less than $10 per capita on the purchase of arms.

TABLE 6
Military Expenditures By
Developing Region, 1973

	1973 Military Expenditures in Constant Dollars			
Region	Amount (billions U.S. $)	As % of GNP	$ Per Capita	(1963-1973) % Growth Rate
Africa	2.1	2.8[a]/	7	6.5[b]/
Latin America	2.9	1.3	8	3.9
Near East	10.1[c]/	11.9[a]/	56[a]/	14.7[b]/
East Asia	19.5	3.4	14	7.5
South Asia	2.4	3.5	3	2.9
OPEC	5.8[c]/	5.7[a]/	16[a]/	11.9[b]/
Developing Countries	32.9	5.6	11	7.2
Developed Countries	208.8	5.7	206	2.0
World	241.7	5.6	62	2.6

Source: Adapted from **World Military Expenditures and Arms Trade, 1963-1973**, U.S. Arms Control and Disarmament Agency, Washington, D.C., 1975, pp. 14-18.
a/ 1972
b/ 1963-1972
c/ Current dollars.

In the 1961-1965 period, the United States was the major arms supplier to the Latin American nations, with the exception of Cuba. By the 1970s, the situation changed radically. France made a large impact in the 1960s by introducing Mirage supersonic fighters after the U.S. Congress refused to permit the sale of such sophisticated warplanes to countries such as Peru. In the first half of the 1960s, the Soviet Union introduced massive amounts of military equipment into Cuba, more than twice the amount the remainder of the world exported to Latin America. By 1975, Cuba had received over $2 billion in Soviet arms. The Russians have also sold smaller amounts to Peru.

Latin America has turned to Western Europe, Canada, and Russia for about 60 percent of its arms imports over the last decade. As Congressional restrictions placed on U.S. arms sales were increased, Western European salesmen moved into Latin America with competitive offerings in the 1960s. Some of this non-U.S. military equipment had serious drawbacks: often it was too expensive, inadequately supplied with spare parts, or too sophisticated for local needs.

Despite these problems, the major Latin American arms purchasing countries have continued their policy of diversifying arms supplies in the 1970s. France and Russia have been the primary suppliers of tanks; the British have provided naval vessels and aircraft; and West Germany has supplied mainly armored vehicles and naval vessels. Canada has increased its sales of subsonic aircraft, while recently U.S.sales of F-5, A-37, and C-130 have surged. And the United States still dominates the helicopter market.

Latin American indigenous arms production is expanding rapidly, with Argentina and Brazil in the lead followed by Peru and Colombia. Aside from light arms that are manufactured or assembled in various countries, such items as jet aircraft, helicopters, destroyers, submarines, tanks, and missiles are manufactured or assembled locally under coproduction or licensing agreements. The volume of intra-Latin American arms trade is still small, but it is on the increase. Brazil is already beginning to export armored personnel carriers, and this may be followed soon by fighter aircraft. This marks the beginning of Latin America's role as an arms supplier to the world market.

The relatively low level of Latin America's expenditures on military equipment reflects the lack of any credible external threat to the individual nations of the region. The absence of any serious military conflict between the Latin American nations for three generations fortifies this perception, although regional military rivalries and revanchist claims continue (such as among such bordering states as Chile, Peru and Bolivia, and Venezuela and Guyana). Latin American armies are primarily oriented toward internal threats, which explains the budgetary emphasis on manpower and the paucity of sophisticated and expensive equipment.

With the recent relaxation of restrictions on U.S. arms sales, Latin America has again turned to North America for much of its weaponry. The desire to avoid complete arms dependence on the United States will undoubtedly encourage Latin American countries to continue making arms purchases from non-hemispheric suppliers.

Cooperative regional efforts to limit and control the buildup of arms have a long and unhappy history. They have had little or no discernable impact on actual arms acquisitions of the countries of the region. The *Declaration of Ayacucho*, signed in Lima in 1974, is the latest effort to restrict the arms race in Latin America. Its value is vitiated by its restricted coverage—the six Andean countries and Argentina and Panama. Major arms purchasers, such as Argentina and Brazil, are not constrained by the Declaration. Furthermore, it is not binding on the Andean countries, and none of them have interrupted their acquisition of new arms and military equipment overseas.

XII. NUCLEAR TECHNOLOGY TRANSFER

The transfer of nuclear technology from the advanced industrial countries to Latin America constitutes an important interface between the region and the world system that has not been examined with the seriousness that it merits. The acquisition of nuclear technology and the spread of fissionable materials increases the probability of nuclear proliferation and the threat to world stability and peace.

At present, no country in Latin America possesses nuclear weapons. But neither Argentina nor Brazil has disguised its intention to build and test nuclear explosives for peaceful purposes most likely before the mid-1980s. The sole distinction between nuclear weapons and peaceful nuclear devices is the intent of the user.

Argentina and Brazil have the two most advanced and sophisticated civil nuclear energy programs—with the greatest military potential—in Latin America. Mexico, Chile, Cuba, and other countries trail far behind. The scope and depth of Argentina's nuclear energy and research program gives it an edge on Brazil, although this situation may well change radically before 1985.

Both countries have been acquiring the scientific and technical knowledge, the nuclear raw materials, and the scientific-technical infrastructure required for the production of nuclear explosives and weapons. They oppose international controls that would limit their research and development programs for the peaceful use of atomic energy or prevent the manufacture of nuclear explosives for peaceful applications.

Argentina possesses the most advanced nuclear energy program in Latin America and it has built five research reactors, one power reactor (Atucha-319 mw), with another (Rio Tercero-600 mw) under construction (see Table 7). The five research reactors are fueled by enriched uranium obtained from the United States and subject to International Atomic Energy Association (IAEA) safeguards. Argentina has far more uranium reserves than any other Latin American country—not only ample for its own needs but also a surplus for occasional export. It intends to develop an ambitious nuclear power program with a nuclear generating capacity of 30,000 mw (30 percent of the national total) by the year 2000. The historic and continuing rivalry between Argentina and Brazil is a factor that contributes substantially to Argentina's desire to gain international status and prestige as a member of the exclusive club of nuclear nations, as well as to provide a counterpoint to Brazil's nuclear expansion.

TABLE 7
Research And Power Reactors In Latin America

	Research	Power
Argentina	5	319 mw Atucha (I.O.)-natural uranium 600 mw Rio Tercero (U.C.)-natural uranium
Brazil	4	626 mw Angra dos Reis (U.C.)-enriched uranium
Mexico	4	660 mw Laguna Verde Ver I (U.C.)-enriched uranium 660 mw Laguna Verde Ver II (U.C.)-enriched uranium
Cuba	1	
Chile	1	
Venezuela	1	
Colombia	1	
Uruguay	1	

I.O. - In Operation
U.C. - Under Construction

Brazil's varied nuclear research program includes four operating research reactors fueled by enriched uranium supplied by the United States, and one power reactor (Angra dos Reis-626 mw) under construction. Its nuclear power program has lagged behind that of Argentina's because of Brazil's vast hydroelectric potential. But Brazil's heavy dependence on expensive oil imports to meet domestic consumption requirements has stimulated a massive national commitment to nuclear power in recent years. Between 1985-1990 it is estimated that at least five nuclear plants will be operating, with as many as eight more under construction.

In June 1975, West Germany signed a $4 billion nuclear technology agreement with Brazil that will provide a uranium enrichment facility, a fuel fabrication unit, nuclear reactors, and a facility for reprocessing spent fuel into plutonium, which can be used to make nuclear weapons. Brazil's agreement to submit to international controls for only part of the "fuel cycle" has aroused fears that West German technology may be used to build nuclear weapons and trigger nuclear proliferation in Latin America. In any event, there is every indication that Brazil is making a comprehensive effort to become preeminent in the nuclear energy field in Latin America. No other country in the hemisphere has taken so strong and public a stance regarding the validity of the peaceful applications of nuclear technology.

The goals of Mexico's nuclear program include the production of low cost nuclear power, the production of potable water, and the production of radioisotopes for use in agriculture, industry, and medicine. Mexico has four small operating research reactors with fuel obtained through the auspices of the IAEA, and small reserves of uranium are available to satisfy immediate national requirements. In particular, Mexico is interested in the production of fresh water from salt water in a cooperative program with the United States, although American interest seems to be lacking at the present time.

The Latin American denuclearization movement has resulted in the 1967 Treaty for Prohibition of Nuclear Weapons (Treaty of Tlatelolco), and the Organization for the Prohibition of Nuclear Weapons (OPANAL). So far Mexico is the only Latin American nation with a nuclear weapons potential to have submitted its entire nuclear program to the safeguard procedures of the IAEA. Other Latin American countries (Chile, Colombia, Peru, Uruguay, Venezuela, and Cuba) have either acquired research reactors or have expressed interest in developing a nuclear research capability.

The Tlatelolco Treaty is a regional version of the Nuclear Non-Proliferation Treaty of 1968, but is more restrictive since it also prohibits the establishment of nuclear weapons bases in Latin America. At present, 22 (out of 24) Latin American states have signed the Treaty, and it is in force in 18 states that have ratified it. OPANAL is considerably weakened by the non-ratification of the Treaty by Argentina and Brazil, and the inadequate financial support from the Treaty signatories.

The concept of a nuclear weapons-free zone for Latin America continues to ba a vulnerable one. For example, Cuba has neither signed nor ratified the Tlatelolco Treaty or the Nuclear Non-Proliferation Treaty. At present Cuba has one nuclear reactor supplied by the Soviet Union, and at the end of 1974 Fidel Castro declared that Cuba would install its first nuclear power reactor by 1980, and another before 1985. While Cuba is a member of the IAEA, it has refused to subject its research reactor to international safeguards. But if Cuba comes to accept its obligations as a cooperative member of the Latin American system and U.S.-Cuban detente proceeds, Cuba might be persuaded by Mexico and the other Latin American countries to sign the Treaty and assume a non-nuclear weapons status.

Apart from the efforts of Latin American governments to develop nuclear explosives, another potentially grave danger to hemispheric peace and security is the possiblity of nuclear theft, extortion, and terrorism. Nuclear installations, particularly in less stable countries, are vulnerable to terrorist activity. Furthermore, sufficient unclassified information now exists to enable well-trained persons, who are able to acquire fissionable material, to construct a relatively small, portable nuclear weapon. And the massive shipments and spread of fissionable materials increases the likelihood that some will fall into the hands of unscrupulous individuals or groups.

International terrorism is on the increase. During the 1967-1973 period, the U.S. Atomic Energy Commission identified more than 400 cases of international terrorism. There are more than fifty well-financed and armed international terrorist groups, five of them in Latin America. Thus, the rise of international terrorism accompanied by the proliferation of fissionable materials further increases the risks of criminal misuse of nuclear technology.

The theft of fissionable material is by no means a remote possibility. In Argentina, there has been at least one case of reported loss of fissionable materials, and an armed terrorist group attacked and briefly held part of the Atucha nuclear power plant in March 1973.

The spread of nuclear technology and fissionable materials in Latin America could pose a serious threat to hemispheric peace and security in the years ahead. Argentina and Brazil have announced that they intend to develop nuclear explosives for peaceful purposes. Both countries are capable of exploding nuclear devices before the mid-1980s. In view of the intense national rivalries, soon after one country exploded a nuclear device domestic pressures would compel the other country to follow suit. Only Mexico seems to be fully aware of the inherent and growing dangers of the accelerated transfer and wider distribution of nuclear technology in Latin America.

There are, of course, no foolproof ways of preventing nuclear proliferation. Nevertheless, new and stronger technical safeguards for the handling, shipment, and storage of nuclear materials must be devised and introduced in Latin America and elsewhere in the world.

XIII. THE LIMITS OF INTERNATIONALISM

The preceding sections have indicated some of the powerful forces at work, some new, some long standing, that are responsible for Latin America's more balanced and open relationship with the world economy and political system in this era of multipolarity and limited detente. It may be useful at this point to present a brief summary of them:

- There is a widespread desire in Latin America to diversify markets and sources of supply of capital and technology in order to promote rapid economic development, reduction of vulnerability to external economic forces, diminishing dependence on the United States, and more international freedom of action.

- The protectionist trend in the United States has led to trade restrictions that have adversely affected the import of some labor-intensive Latin American manufactured goods, such as textiles and footwear. Affected countries, such as Brazil whose shoe exports were subject to restrictions in U.S. markets, seek markets elsewhere.

- The preferential trading arrangements between the EEC (European Economic Community) and the less developed countries of Africa and Asia discriminate against Latin American exports of raw materials and tropical commodities. The result is an intensified search for new markets outside of the EEC.

- Soviet-American detente and the partial relaxation of East-West tensions in the early 1970s have encouraged a broadening of diplomatic and economic relations between the Latin American countries and the socialist states. The establishment of relations with the Soviet Union, Cuba, and other socialist states is advertised by some Latin American governments as a gesture of "independence" from the United States, which sometimes is politically useful at home.

- The success of the Organization of Petroleum Exporting Countries (OPEC) in raising oil prices also provided a powerful stimulus to mineral and tropical commodity exporting countries in Latin America to attempt to establish their own cartels and producer associations with other countries in Africa and Asia with the aim of regulating supply, raising export prices, and increasing foreign exchange earnings. This resulted in closer contact between the food and mineral exporting countries of Latin America and the Third World and renewed efforts to create producer associations and cartels.

- By contributing to the balance of payments pressures of the net oil importing countries in Latin America, whose primary commodity (such as sugar, cacao, coffee, copper) export prices entered a new period of decline in 1975, OPEC has generated additional pressures on oil-importing countries to seek new markets and to diversify exports.

- Some regional political leaders believe that Latin American and Third World unity can create irresistible pressures on the industrial world to meet their political and economic demands, and ultimately to restructure the international economic system in their favor. Therefore, these Latin American leaders are making a considerable effort to establish close and regular political consultation and cooperation with various groups of developing countries such as the so-called non-aligned movement.

- The emergence of the Middle Eastern oil exporting countries as major net exporters of capital has led to the establishment of completely new financial and economic relations on the part of some Latin American countries (notably Brazil and Argentina) during the past few years.

- In some countries, such as Brazil (with its Japanese ethnic minority and African cultural heritage) and Guyana (with African and Asian ethnic roots), new political and commercial relations have been created with Third World countries based on ethnic bonds.

- The revolutions in global transportation and communications have made the remote areas of the world more accessible to the Latin American countries, thereby facilitating the interchange of goods, services, and people.

A review of Latin America's political and commercial opening up to non-traditional areas—in Asia, Africa, the Middle East, and the socialist camp—indicates that the intensified political interaction has not been accompanied by any radical reorientation of the region's international economic relations, which are still concentrated on the North Atlantic (United States, Canada, and Western Europe) trading area. The only exception is Japan, which is rapidly emerging as a major new economic partner for a growing number of Latin American countries. Japanese-Latin American commercial flows may ultimately rival those of the United States and Western Europe before the end of the century.

Parts of Latin America have also drawn closer economically to Eastern Europe, and to a lesser extent to Russia. Even Cuba's heavy dependence on the Soviet Union (and the socialist camp) for trade and aid is giving way to more diversified economic relations with the free market economies of the Western Hemisphere and Western Europe. Cuban-Canadian commercial relations, starting from a low base, have also grown substantially in the seventies. Regional members of raw material cartels or producer associations (such as Venezuela and Ecuador in OPEC, Peru and Chile in CIPEC, Jamaica and Guyana in IBA) have also formed close functional bonds with other Third World producers in Africa, the Middle East, and Asia.

There are, however, obvious limits to this process of diversification of Latin America's political and economic relations on a global scale. A crucial fact is that the North Atlantic area plus Japan will dominate the world economy for the remainder of this century. Presently accounting for about 70 percent of world trade and about 60 percent of world GNP, the North Atlantic-Japanese trading area will account for an even larger share of world trade by 1980, and its share of world GNP will not be much lower. This vast trading area will continue to offer the Latin American countries their major markets for their traditional mineral and agricultural exports—and increasingly for their manufactured goods—for the remainder of the century. Inevitably it will be the dominant supplier of development finance, new technology, management skills, machinery, and equipment essential for Latin America's further economic transformation.

Another crucial fact is that geography, climate, natural resources, demography, and levels of technology and skill impose powerful constraints—as Castro's Cuba has discovered—on the extent to which the Latin American countries, particularly the smaller Caribbean republics, are able to establish lasting and significant economic relations with new regions outside of the Western Hemisphere and North Atlantic area. As the natural limits to effective diversification of relations are reached over the next decade, the superficiality of Latin American voluntarist orthodoxies (the belief that the Latin masses are infinitely malleable, that political will is all that is needed to transform societies and drastically alter old economic relationships) will become manifest.

For some time it has been evident that the international system has entered a period of redefinition and significant adjustment. In the forefront of these changes has been the insertion of Latin America into the world economy and deeper involvement in the world political agenda—commodities, technology transfer, multinational corporations, and nuclear proliferation. This inexorable historical process clearly offers new opportunities for constructive cooperation between the Latin American countries and their traditional political and economic partners in North America and Western Europe. What is less certain is whether the imagination and pragmatism exist to take advantage of the opportunity to build a new, closer political and economic relationship between North America, Western Europe, and Japan. For these regions—whatever their differences and however imperfectly—share a common political tradition and a common cultural heritage that respects human rights and personal freedoms.

Despite the steps taken by the Latin American countries to intensify their relations with other regions, the magnitude and conditions of the flow of trade, aid, capital, and technology from the United States, Western Europe (and increasingly Japan) still occupy the central focus of Latin America's international politics and economic interests. The dominant reality is that the prosperity of the Latin American countries continues to be bound together with that of the North Atlantic area, and this situation can be expected to prevail at least until the end of the twentieth century.

NOTES

1. Economic integration can take many forms that represent varying degrees of integration, ranging from a free trade area, through complete economic integration. In a free trade area, tariffs and quantitative restrictions are abolished between member countries but each state retains its own tariffs against nonmembers. A customs union is, in effect, a free trade area which established equal tariffs in trade with nonmembers. A higher form of integration is a common market which not only abolished restrictions on trade but also on factors movements between member states. Total economic integration implies the unification of economic and social policies and the creation of a supranational authority capable of imposing binding decisions on all members.

2. The Andean Community members are: Bolivia, Chile, Ecuador, Peru, Colombia, and Venezuela.

3. The eleven countries that established AIOPEC are: Algeria, Australia, Chile, India, Mauritania, Peru, Philippines, Sierra Leone, Sweden, Tunisia, and Venezuela. Liberia and Brazil are expected to become members soon.

4. The EEC also provides compensatory trade assistance under the Lomé Agreement. The EEC provides compensation to countries whose raw material export values fall below the average for the four prior years. For sugar, the EEC import price is negotiated each year, and the import quota has been set for 1.2 million metric tons in 1975, and 1.4 million metric tons for future years.

5. Cuba is a special case not included in the discussion of Latin America in this chapter because it is part of the Soviet bloc and a ward of the Soviet Union.

6. See U.S. Commission for Latin America Report: El Desarrollo Latinoamericano y la Coyuntura Economica Internacional (E/CEPAL/981) Vol. I, 1975.

REFERENCES

BEMIS, SAMUEL F. (1943) The Latin American Policy of the United States. New York: Harcourt, Brace & World.
CARNOY, MARTIN (1972) Industrialization in a Latin American Common Market. Washington, D.C.: The Brookings Institution.
CLISSOLD, STEPHEN [ed.] (1970) Soviet Relations with Latin America, 1918-1968. London: Oxford Univ. Press.
GOLDHAMER, HERBERT (1972) The Foreign Powers in Latin America. Princeton: Princeton Univ. Press.
GRUNWALD, JOSEPH and PHILIP MUSGROVE [eds.] (1970) Natural Resources in Latin American Development. Baltimore: Johns Hopkins Univ. Press.
GRUNWALD, JOSEPH, MIGUEL S. WIONCZEK, and MARTIN CARNOY (1972) Latin American Integration and U.S. Policy. Washington, D.C.: The Brookings Institution.
HIRSCHMAN, ALBERT O. (1971) A Bias for Hope. New Haven: Yale Univ. Press.
OHARA, YOSHINORI (1967) Japan and Latin America. Santa Monica RAND Corp. Memorandum, RM-5388-Rc, November.
REDICK, JOHN (1975) Regional Nuclear Arms Control in Latin America. International Organization, Summer.
SCHNEIDER, RONALD M. (1971) The Political System of Brazil. New York: Columbia Univ. Press.

A000014631894

Subscribers to *The Washington Papers* are entitled to a special 20 percent discount on all of the following CSIS publications. Orders must refer to *Washington Paper* subscription to qualify and be prepaid to: Georgetown Center for Strategic and International Studies, 1800 K St. NW, Washington, DC 20006.

	The 1975 CSIS Quadrangular (Quad II) Conference:	List Price	Discount Price
1.	**Interrelationship of Inflation/Recession, the International Financial Structure, and Alliance Security,** rapporteur E. Luttwak (1975); 63 pp.,	$3.95	$3.15
2.	**Commissioned Papers on Inflation/Recession—Quad II,** H. Block and H. Johnson (1975); 66 pp.,	$5.00	$4.00
3.	**Selected Papers on Inflation/Recession—Quad II,** ed. by P. Hartland-Thunberg (1975); 156 pp.,	$5.00	$4.00
4.	**International Information, Education, and Cultural Relations: Recommendations for the Future,** panel with F. Stanton et al. (1975); 96 pp.,	$3.95	$3.15
5.	**Soviet-United States Naval Balance,** R. Kilmarx (1975); 187 pp.,	$5.00	$4.00
6.	**Western World under Economic Stress,** P. Hartland-Thunberg (1975); 14 pp.,	$1.50	$1.20
7.	**The Soviet Union and the Western Crisis,** W. Laqueur et al. (1975); 31 pp.,	$4.00	$3.15
8.	**Freedom in the Third World,** T. Sumberg (1975); 91 pp.,	$5.00	$4.00
9.	**The Economic Prospects of the Persian Gulf Amirates,** F. K. Lundy (1974); 95 pp.,	$5.00	$4.00
10.	**The International Relations of Southern Africa,** ed. by C. Crocker (1974); 113 pp.,	$2.50	$2.00
11.	**Commercial Diplomacy,** by L. Barrows (1974); 128 pp.,	$5.00	$4.00

Special 20 percent discount on CSIS publications to all Washington Paper subscribers

THIS VOLUME FOR USE IN THE LIBRARY ONLY AND CANNOT BE CHECKED OUT.